W9-AES-538

LOUIS PASTEUR

by Beverley Birch

Picture Credits

Anthony Blake Photo Library, p. 42; Bridgeman Art Library, pp. 9, 34-35, 43; John Cleare, p. 4; CNRI, p. 53 (below); Mary Evans Picture Library, pp. 8, 41; Exley Photographic Library: Nick Birch, pp. 12 (left), 16 (below, both), 30, 31 (above), 35 (below), 38, 57 (both); Giraudon, front cover, pp. 19, 26; Giraudon, Musée des Beaux-Arts, Nantes, p. 25; Georges Goldner, pp. 16 (above), 58 (below), 59; Eric Grave, pp. 12-13, 53 (above); Hulton Picture Library, pp. 40 (above), 45, 51; Illustrated London News, p. 11; The Mansell Collection, p. 55; Oxford Scientific Films: G. I. Bernard, p. 47 (all); Pasteur Institute, pp. 5, 15, 36, 40 (below), 61; Roger-Viollet, pp. 50, 56; Ann Ronan Picture Library, pp. 21, 28, 29, 44, 46 (all), 49, 54, 58 (above); David Scharf, p. 23; Science Photo Library, pp. 7, 20, 31 (below); Sinclair Stammers, p. 22; John Walsh, p. 33, 39.

North American edition first published in 1989 by
Gareth Stevens, Inc.
7317 West Green Tree Road
Milwaukee, WI 53223 USA

First published in the United Kingdom in 1989
© 1989 by Exley Publications Ltd.
Text © 1989 by Beverley Birch
Additional end matter © 1989 by Gareth Stevens, Inc.

Library of Congress Cataloging-in-Publication Data

Birch, Beverley.
　　Louis Pasteur.

　　(People who have helped the world)
　　Includes index.
　　Summary: A biography of the nineteenth-century French scientist who discovered the process for destroying harmful bacteria with heat and opened the door to the new science of microbiology.
　　1. Pasteur, Louis, 1822-1895--Juvenile literature.
2. Microbiologists--France--Biography--Juvenile literature. 3. Scientists--France--Biography--Juvenile literature. [1. Pasteur, Louis, 1822-1895. 2. Microbiologists. 3. Scientists] I. Title. II. Series.
Q143.P2B57　1989　576'.092'4　[B]　[92]　　88-24867
ISBN 1-55532-839-3

Series conceived and edited by Helen Exley
Picture research: Karen Gunnell
Editorial: Margaret Montgomery
Editor, U.S.: Rita Reitci
Editorial assistant, U.S.: Scott Enk

Printed in Hungary

1 2 3 4 5 6 7 8 9 94 93 92 91 90 89

LOUIS PASTEUR.

The scientist who discovered the cause of infectious disease and invented pasteurization

by Beverley Birch

Gareth Stevens Children's Books
MILWAUKEE

Left: Mont Blanc in the Alps, to which Pasteur traveled in order to collect air samples.

Right: Pasteur collecting mountain air in an S-necked flask containing broth.

The hunt for pure air

The procession wound its slow path up the mountain, the surefooted guides moving ahead on the stony track. Behind, the mule swayed beneath a load of strange, bulbous bottles.

Around the plodding animal another man, a small man with glasses, eagerly ran this way and that. He checked the harness and guided the animal anxiously along the edge of the precipice in the mistaken belief that he was less likely to slither off the narrow path than the sturdy little mule was.

Up and up they toiled to the glinting peaks of snowy Mont Blanc. They sniffed the air with excitement. They climbed on in the morning sunshine and, at last, onto the white, untrodden snows of the Mer de Glace, the Sea of Ice.

And here, on this great glacier, a strange kind of ceremony began. The man lit a lamp, a lamp with a powerful, jetlike flame. Delicately he removed a bottle from its cradle on the mule's back. It was not an ordinary bottle, but a plump round-bellied flask with a straight, narrow neck tapering to a point.

He held it above his head. Inside was a clear liquid that caught the light from snow and ice and sparkled.

With a pair of steel pincers, he snapped off the tip of the fine glass neck—then, a sharp hiss, as air rushed through the narrow opening into the belly of the flask. Then almost immediately he took the lamp and ran its flame to and fro across the opening so that the glass melted and the opening sealed again.

He took up the second flask: snap, that telltale hiss of air. Swiftly the flame played across the opening. Then the third flask, the fourth, the fifth . . . each in turn, until twenty flasks had been opened and closed again.

He beamed. They all beamed with him. Success!

It had to be right

Yesterday they had failed. They had toiled up that same path to that same glacier to perform the same ceremony. But yesterday it had gone wrong.

Everything had gone according to plan until the moment came to seal the neck of the first flask with the lamp. Against the brilliance of the sky and glaring snow, it was impossible to see the flame! And the wind whipped it to and fro so there was no hope of aiming it at the open neck of the flask.

Only one answer: abandon the task and retrace their steps, find a tinsmith in the village of Chamonix at the foot of the mountain. Get him to make a lamp that could give off a steady flame. Everything must be done exactly right. The flasks must be open for only an instant, to let in the mountain air, and then closed again.

The great debate

You may well wonder what was happening on that icy morning on the Mer de Glace. Louis Pasteur was proving something. Louis Pasteur was doing a precise and brilliantly simple scientific experiment. He was going to settle, once and for all, one of the major questions of science.

For weeks he and his assistants had been preparing: cleaning flasks, making the liquid to put in them, boiling them, sealing them, packing them for their journeys. Some were carried across Paris to dank cellars or dusty yards, others were hoisted up a hill near Pasteur's hometown of Arbois, and others were nursed carefully on the train journey to the Alps for their voyage up Mont Blanc.

Louis Pasteur was trying to prove something, and when Louis Pasteur looked for proof, he left nothing to chance.

"Always doubt yourself, till the facts cannot be doubted," Pasteur said. And there lies the secret of his enormous contribution to the world. However brilliant the idea, it is no good unless it works, so test and test again, with attention to the tiniest of details, until there can be no question of any mistake.

There are a number of rather loose claims about Pasteur's work. He is said to have invented everything

"Crystals — fermentation — spontaneous generation — wine — silkworms — beer — vaccines — rabies."
Inscription in the chapel of the Pasteur Institute

"Let me tell you the secret that has led me to the goal. My only strength resides in my tenacity."
Louis Pasteur

6

from the smallest detail, like the special swan-necked flasks used in his early experiments, to the painstaking experiments that proved the truth of the germ theory of disease.

This theory proposes that germs, those microscopic creatures known to us as microbes, are the cause of many diseases. But to heap vague and often inaccurate claims like this upon him is to obscure the man's real gigantic contribution to science and medicine.

Some of the scientific observations and ideas that Pasteur tackled had been around for a long time, some for two hundred years — since the first microscope revealed that vast world of tiny creatures that came to be known as microbes. But for all the notice scientists took of early observations about microbes, it was just as if Pasteur were the first.

The key to understanding disease

He certainly rediscovered things that some earlier scientists had already discovered. But Pasteur went further. He confirmed old facts about microbes and discovered new ones, but he also saw how they were all related to each other.

He made that visionary flight into understanding — not just microbes as fascinating things, but microbes as the root of many life processes of the world. Then he traced it by painstaking and imaginative experiment.

He made that inspired leap from seeing how microbes live and die to realizing that here was the key to understanding disease. He became a prophet whose vision shot the scientists of his time forward into a revolutionary perception of the birth, life, decay, and death of matter.

Armed with this perception, they were able to unlock the secrets of disease. Doctors became not merely people who helped others to endure and perhaps survive disease. They became those who cured and prevented illnesses that had been the scourge of the human race for thousands of years.

In the decades that followed, discovery led to discovery. Whole new sciences emerged as new findings gave birth to new questions. The first was

"I am the most hesitating of men, the most fearful of committing myself when I lack evidence. But on the contrary, no consideration can keep me from defending what I hold as true when I can rely on solid scientific evidence."
Louis Pasteur

Fifteenth-century woodcut of a man dying from plague. The doctor wards off the "evil emanations" by holding to his nose a sponge soaked in a preparation of herbs. The Black Death plague of the 1300s killed up to half the population of Europe.

the science of microbiology. Another was the scientific study of the cause, control, and prevention of disease — not least through inoculation and immunization. These are the techniques that encourage the body to develop its own immunity to microbes. And there was also asepsis, the practice of the controlling and destroying of germs in hospitals, particularly during surgery.

Pasteur and those he trained were in the forefront of this great movement in science and medicine. Their work revolutionized medical practice.

And their discoveries were an inspiration to scientists and doctors throughout the world, an influence whose scale is so vast that it can never be fully measured.

And as he galloped down this path, on the way Pasteur rescued whole industries from disaster — possibly from extinction — with his painstaking research on silkworms, wine and beer, and cattle and sheep disease.

Today we take for granted the technique of pasteurization, the technique that bears his name and that most often reminds us of him. Every day, dairies free our milk from disease-causing germs using this remarkable process.

Right: An early picture of Paris showing the crowded, damp, and filthy conditions that allowed infectious diseases to flourish. Cholera, typhoid, pneumonia, diphtheria, plague, tuberculosis, and syphilis were common and often spread from slums like this to other areas.

Opposite: Often in earlier times women died in childbirth from infections and children died in infancy. It was common for a family to lose two or three children to disease. (Artist: Henry Jules Jean Geoffroy, 1853-1924)

8

Enemies

Not surprisingly, he provoked enemies. His work, particularly as a standard-bearer of the germ theory of disease, disproved some long-held theories. And such was his conviction that he rode roughshod over those who refused to respond to the truth of his research or who picked holes in his results.

With hindsight, and the greater knowledge of modern science, we can see that there were some holes to be found. But how few holes compared to the enormous forward march of science and medicine, a march that Pasteur's work was to help inspire!

So what was he trying to prove on that glacier on Mont Blanc? It was something that is so commonplace to us now that one wonders why, for over a hundred years, scientists had been arguing about it. It was quite simply the question of whether there are germs in the air.

It is perhaps hard now to think of this as a revolutionary idea, for in our everyday life we accept it by using soaps and antiseptic cleaners, by cleaning and dressing wounds, and by performing operations in germ-free conditions with germ-free instruments.

We now know that there are microscopic living organisms on and in everything in the world: on solid matter, in the dusts of the air, and in water and other liquids. We know that some of these microorganisms do essential tasks for us: they make waste materials decay to provide food for plant life, they turn raw materials into bread or wine, and some even take part in the digestive process in our bodies. We also know that others cause fatal disease when they enter the human, animal, or plant body, killing people or animals in the millions.

None of this was known when Pasteur began probing into the mysteries of germs. All that was known was that these creatures existed.

We have Anton van Leeuwenhoek, a Dutchman who died a hundred years before Pasteur was born, to thank for that. Leeuwenhoek had an enormous curiosity about the world around him. He wanted to find out what things really looked like, and he heard that a magnifying lens would help. So he set out to learn how to grind and polish lenses and began a life

"I have taken my drop of water . . . full of elements most suited to the development of small beings. And I wait, I observe, I question it, I beg it to be so kind as to begin over again just to please me, the primitive act of creation; it would be so fair a sight! But it is mute! It has been mute for years. Ah! That is because I . . . have kept from it the germs that float in the air; I have kept it from life, for life is a germ and a germ is life. Never will the belief in spontaneous generation arise from the mortal blow that this simple experiment has given it."

Pasteur, in a public lecture at the Sorbonne

10

of peering and sniffing and poking at everything he could lay his hands on, just to find out. Skin, hair, seeds, insects, tree bark, and the cavities of rotten teeth were all subjects of the prying glint of his lenses!

The microscope

In fact, he had invented what we call the microscope. And from his quiet life in a small Dutch town toward the end of the seventeenth century, he set the world on fire. For the first time, people realized there was this world of creatures so tiny that they were invisible to the naked eye.

Peering one day through one of his magnifying lenses, he was transfixed by the sight of millions of tiny creatures in the rainwater in his yard! How they slithered and wriggled. No matter how long he watched them, they never stopped. Millions of them, a thousand times smaller even than the eye of a large louse (and a whole louse is too small to be seen in any detail with the naked eye).

Everything he looked at was swarming with these tiny creatures. He did not make guesses about what

A cholera epidemic in Granada, Spain, 1887. People are burning tar and sulfur in an attempt to disinfect the streets. On the left, a street party is collecting a patient to take to the hospital. Up to five hundred people died each day during the worst of the epidemic.

11

The last microscope that Pasteur used. The microscope was at the heart of his work. Invented in the seventeenth century by Leeuwenhoek, it was transformed by Pasteur from a means of observation into an important instrument in the fight against disease.

they were doing, and it never entered his head that they were causing anything, least of all decay or disease. But he did discover that they were killed by heat. One day he was squinting at scrapings from his own teeth and found that after he'd drunk scalding hot coffee, the tiny creatures were either dead or very sluggish.

He wrote his findings down and sent long descriptions to scientists in England. They had recently formed the Royal Society in order to exchange scientific ideas and learn from each other. He told them he could *grow* these creatures in water mixed with pepper: one drop of pepper-water held more than 2,700,000! They built microscopes, repeated his experiments, and found he told the truth.

Spallanzani's work on microbes

But after Leeuwenhoek's discoveries and that first excitement, the little creatures were on the brink of being forgotten again. Then, when Leeuwenhoek was dead and the eighteenth century was well past the halfway mark, an Italian priest named Lazzaro Spallanzani, a professor at the University of Reggio

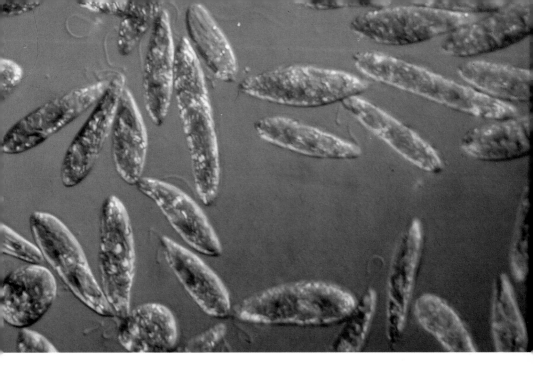

in Italy, became fascinated by the wiggling microscopic beings.

In Spallanzani's time, there was a great debate going on. It was the same debate that, about one hundred years later, would fire Louis Pasteur into the front line of battle, as its fierce warrior, to settle the matter once and for all.

The question was this: Does every living thing have to have parents, or can living things spring into life spontaneously? The argument was bound up with beliefs about how the world was first formed.

A photomicrograph of the kind of microorganism Leeuwenhoek might have seen in stagnant water with his microscope. These single-cell organisms are flagellates.

Spontaneous life?

The idea popular in Spallanzani's day, to remain so until Pasteur laid it to rest, was that things came alive spontaneously. If you buried the carcass of a bull, so the story went, out would pop a spontaneously generated swarm of bees! Wasps and beetles would emerge out of dung, mice and frogs would slither from the slime of riverbanks, and maggots would crawl from meat.

Spallanzani thought this whole idea was ridiculous. But how could he show he was right? One day he read the writings of a man named Francesco Redi, who had proved that flies had to reach meat for the maggots to appear and that if you stopped flies from getting to the meat, by covering it, there would be no maggots!

Spallanzani was entranced by the simplicity of this — not to just observe, but to experiment, to find proof. So he began his experiments and showed that the tiny living creatures we now call microbes do not arise spontaneously, that when you find them on things or in liquids it is because they have reached there from somewhere else.

He did an experiment very like one Pasteur devised many years later to prove the same point. He boiled soups of seeds and beans for an hour to kill all microbes, sealed the necks of the flasks by melting the glass, and showed that no new microbes appeared inside the flasks. They could not enter because of the sealed neck.

Microbes divide

He read that a Swiss scientist named Horace Bénédict de Saussure had seen that microbes increased by multiplying. Each one split into two, and those two into four, and so on.

Enchanted by this idea, Spallanzani found a way to trap one in a drop of distilled water and then watched it through the microscope until he actually saw it happening. The tiny rodlike shape got thinner and thinner in the middle until it became two small rods held together by no more than a cobweb-thin thread! Some frantic jerks and wriggles later, they had pulled apart before his eyes and were two rodlike creatures. And then it happened again! Each one grew thin in the middle. . . .

But in the end, in spite of the excitement that Spallanzani's work caused in the learned societies of Europe, the novelty of peering into this world of the infinitely small wore off. No one learned much that was new, and interest in the creatures faded. As the years went by, those old theories that Spallanzani had worked so hard to bury, the theories about the spontaneous generation of living things, reared their argumentative heads again.

And then the germ theory

Then came Louis Pasteur in France. Within thirty years, the knowledge of the world was transformed. Pasteur, with his passionate convictions and meticulous experiments, propelled scientists from the darkness of prejudice and confused half-knowledge into the daylight in which all the techniques of modern preventive medicine could be born.

Louis Pasteur unquestionably proved, and scientists grasped the idea, that the germs of microbes do not arise spontaneously but travel into things (liquids and foods, for instance) from outside, for example, in the dust of air. Once he'd done that, the way was open to proving the germ theory of disease — that much disease is caused by the invasion of the human, animal, or plant body by microbes that overwhelm and weaken it.

Young Louis Pasteur as a student at the École Normale Supérieure. His ambition was to become a teacher.

The scientists of Pasteur's day were not slow to realize that if microbes caused many diseases, then the microbes must be tracked and caught. Ways must be found of controlling, killing, or preventing them from taking hold. The era of immunology was born, the knowledge of how to make the body develop its own defenses against the microbes of specific diseases.

How many countless lives have been saved by this great movement in medicine in which Pasteur was one of the prime movers! He was a great inspirer of other great scientists who have worked to clear the world of the diseases that only a little more than a hundred years ago wiped out people by the hundreds of thousands each year.

To appreciate this revolutionary contribution to the world, we need to go back to Louis Pasteur's beginnings to trace the story as he and his fellow workers saw it and as the world saw it at the time.

Pasteur the boy

The early life of Louis Pasteur is remarkable for the absence of anything to warn us that he was going to be a scientist. He showed no particular early interest in science, nor was there anything to give us a clue that he would become an explorer, a searcher for some of the fundamental secrets of life, or a man with so strong a sense of mission.

15

Above: Arbois, where Louis grew up in a house on the banks of the Cuisance River. It remained his retreat throughout his life.

Right and below: Louis did these portraits in pastels of his father and his mother when he was a teenager. They hang in the Pasteur Institute in Paris. Louis loved to draw. At age thirteen, he showed considerable talent.

His talents seemed mainly in drawing and painting. At the age of thirteen, he showed a remarkable skill in painting pictures of his sisters and mother and in drawing the river that ran by his home in Arbois.

He grew up in that part of France that is not far from Switzerland and the Alps, in the area of the Jura Mountains that forms a rugged barrier between the two countries. In the small town of Dôle, on the Doubs River, he was born on December 27, 1822, in a house on a street that now bears his name. But in 1822 it was called the rue des Tanneurs, "the street of the tanners." Each house was a tannery where fresh skins of cattle and sheep were tanned, turned into leather. Louis' father, an old sergeant from the armies of Napoleon Bonaparte, was a tanner.

But Louis was little more than two years old when he and his sisters were loaded into a cart with their furniture and their father's tools to make the journey to nearby Marnoz. In 1827, they settled in the town of Arbois, snug amid its wooded hills. Here there was a tannery, a house with pits in the yard where the skins could be soaked, a room where his father could sell leather, another for his workshop, and space above where the family could live.

Here, with his three sisters, Louis grew up in hilly Arbois with its plane trees and poplars, its squares and shady arcades, its little Cuisance River running by the wall of his house and splashing under the bridge, and its nearby fields where small boys could play and fish endlessly. This town remained the focus of his young life for many years.

To Paris

He seems to have developed one overriding, early ambition — to become a teacher. He wanted to go to Paris to study at the École Normale Supérieure, a school founded by Napoleon to train professors for the schools and colleges of France.

But Louis' first attempt at studying in Paris was disastrous. He was not yet sixteen, and the bonds that held him to his family were too strong. Plucked from the familiar haunts of his country life and plunged over 250 miles (400 km) away into the crowded streets and looming houses of Paris, Louis was crippled with homesickness. He did not see the excitement of the Latin Quarter, the students thronging the university of the Sorbonne, and pavement cafés humming with young people. He felt only the difference and the loneliness.

The experiment lasted only about a month before his father made the long journey by stagecoach to fetch him home again. Back went Louis to the college at Arbois and back to his drawings and paintings. He began producing a remarkable set of pastel portraits of friends and acquaintances. Later, Louis went to college in Besançon, only about twenty-five miles (40 km) away. There he seems to have flourished, to have been happy and much praised for his drawings.

But he seems never to have lost sight of his goal. At Besançon he began to prepare for the École Normale. He was not content with his first results in the entrance exam, for though he was accepted, he placed fifteenth among the twenty-two applicants. He decided to leave Besançon, study for another year, and try again.

Paris again

So Louis went back to Paris, and this was very different from his first miserable experience. Here was a Louis determined and ready to reach his goal. He lived at the Barbet boarding school, the same place where he had become so homesick just months earlier. Here he was a teacher as well as a student, rising early to give lessons to the younger boys from six until seven in the morning.

And then the day began with other lessons at the famous school called the Lycée St. Louis. And afterward came the jewels of his day, those lectures at the university of the Sorbonne.

It is about now that we can detect the seeds of Louis' future taking root. We find him passing through the great halls of the Sorbonne amid crowds of six or seven hundred students, all chattering about the latest lecture. And we find Louis spellbound by the vistas opening before him.

What a lecturer this chemistry professor, Monsieur Jean-Baptisté Dumas, was! What a world of

Jean Béraud 1889

fascination he opened up! Louis wrote excited letters home about these lectures, and it seems as if the grip of that first excitement never left him, nor the friendship of Professor Dumas.

At the end of the school year, Louis placed fourth in the entrance exam for the École Normale. He was so eager to begin that he arrived before the beginning of the term. So in October 1843, shortly before his twenty-first birthday, Louis entered the École Normale to learn how to teach chemistry and physics.

When Louis first went to Paris to study, the busy streets and bustling ways seemed strange and unfriendly. He grew to like the city upon his return a year later. As a scientist and teacher, he spent most of his working life here.

First explorations on his own

Microbes couldn't have been further from his mind as he came to the end of his studies at the École Normale and looked around for something special to study, something to give him a chance for a bit of independent exploration.

He must become an excellent teacher: his heart was set on it! He must understand everything he would teach so thoroughly that he could fire youngsters with enthusiasm, just as Professor Dumas captured him during those lectures at the Sorbonne. And perhaps it was his artist's eye that drew him to crystals; they are such delicately intricate fragments.

To Louis' fascination, one of his teachers had shown him a specimen of a salt that had formed crystals. Although it was apparently a very pure salt, it was actually a mixture of three different shapes of crystals. Louis was intrigued. Why three? There must be some purpose. A thousand questions buzzed in his brain, searching for some reason why nature arranged things like this.

And like every scientist since the dawn of our search to know the world around us, he was in his own way launched on two fundamental questions in science: What are substances made of and can we figure out how matter is built?

Crystals and light

Crystals had attracted the attention of the curious for thousands of years. By Louis' time scientists knew a lot about what they looked like, but not a great deal more. A great French physicist, Professor Jean-Baptisté Biot, had also found out that if a beam of light is shone through some crystals, the beam of light doesn't continue in the same straight path; it bends.

Why? Louis was even more intrigued. You must remember that this was long before scientists had worked out how the building blocks of substances — what we call the atoms — are arranged in each substance. It was nearly two decades before they were able to understand how a group of atoms is arranged to form a molecule, and how molecules, in turn, make up the substance — a solid, gas, or liquid. And it was more than half a century before the discovery of radioactivity began to reveal the inner structure of the atom.

So the fact that crystals did unexpected things with beams of light was interesting. It made Louis wonder if there was a link between the kind of crystal and what it did to light. Or between the crystal's chemical composition — its combination of ingredients, what scientists call its compounds — and what it did to light. Or between its shape and what it did to light. There was enough new here to take him well off into

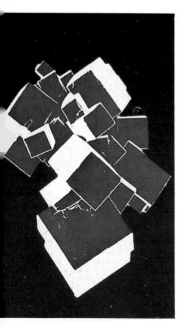

Crystals of table salt, magnified by electron microscope to show their characteristic cubic shape. Louis Pasteur became interested in the crystals of other kinds of salts, the tartrates. His study of their facets laid the foundation of stereochemistry.

uncharted territory. He began making a careful study of a very beautiful series of compounds called tartaric acid and the tartrates. Two forms of tartaric acid crystals were found in the encrustations that build up inside wine barrels while grape juice ferments. But there was a mystery: if you made a solution with the first type of crystal in water, it bent a beam of light, as Professor Biot had seen.

But if you made a water solution with the second type of crystal, it did not bend the beam of light! Yet both crystals were identical chemically; that is, they were made up of the same ingredients.

The first adventure

There must be something here; Louis' developing explorer's nose could scent it! And off he went on this first of his adventures, prodding and picking over piles of crystals, looking at them first this way, then that through his magnifying glass, measuring the angles between the different faces, dissolving them, forming them again, and struggling to find something that would explain this extraordinary difference in what they did to light.

Jean-Baptisté Dumas (1800-1884), Professor of Chemistry at the Sorbonne and Louis' lifelong friend.

He couldn't find it. But with what determination he pressed on, beyond the point where many young scientists in their first piece of research would have given in to weary disenchantment.

The first discovery

And he found himself in the middle of his first great discovery. Peering for the thousandth time through his magnifying glass, he was struck by the fact that the crystals which treated light so differently were the same in all but one respect. The difference was so subtle that he hadn't seen it before! All the faces, or facets, of the two kinds of crystal were identical — except one. In one form of the crystal, one of the facets sloped only one way. In the other, it sloped either way.

With mounting excitement, he separated the two crystals of the second form. He dissolved the different crystals separately in solutions of water and predicted what each would do to a beam of light. Was he going to be right? He hardly dared hope!

Tartaric acid crystals magnified eighty times.

He was! With a burst of glee, he realized what he'd discovered and rushed to tell someone else.

What was so important in all this about acids and the facets of crystals and the beam of light? It meant something very significant, for it showed to Louis that you could study the structure of a crystal by studying what it did with a beam of light; that investigating how a crystal behaved could tell you something about how it was built!

In those days when the investigation of how substances are built was still in its infancy, it was as though a gate opened. Louis' discovery suggested new methods, new techniques, and a whole new approach. In the following years, Louis was busily engaged in this work, in effect laying the foundations of a new science, the science of stereochemistry.

So Louis' discovery was a scientific leap of some significance. And it singled out the young man as an explorer of quality with not only the determination and methodical persistence of an excellent scientist but also the glorious instincts of an adventurer.

"He continued his work on crystals; he did strange and foolish and impossible experiments. . . . He tried to change the chemistry of living things by putting them between huge magnets. He devised weird clockworks that swung plants back and forward, hoping so to change the mysterious molecules that formed these plants into mirror images of themselves. . . ."
Paul de Kruif,
Microbe Hunters

All kinds of other questions buzzed in Louis' brain. These crystals were alike, except that they were mirror images of each other. Again, he asked, why? There was a reason for this difference, which scientists now call dissymmetry. Nature used it in some way, but what way?

These questions were to absorb Louis happily for the next ten years, until an unexpected turn of events propelled him from the world of crystals into the world of another, quite different phenomenon.

Madame Pasteur

By the end of 1848, Louis' time at the École Normale was over, and by January of 1849, he was installed in his first big job as lecturer in chemistry at the University of Strasbourg. It was here, at the age of twenty-six, that he met and fell in love with Marie Laurent, daughter of the university rector.

Fifteen days later, with that determination so characteristic of Louis, he wrote to the rector, asking him for Marie's hand in marriage. "My family is comfortable, but not rich," he wrote. "All we possess is not worth more than fifty thousand francs, and I have long ago decided to let my sisters have it all. . . . All I possess is good health, a willing spirit, and my work.

"I have been a Doctor of Science for eighteen months and I have presented a few works to the Academy of Sciences that have been well received," he wrote. "As to the future, all I can say is that, unless my tastes change entirely, I shall devote myself to chemical research."

He seems to have felt that Marie's mother needed persuading, for he wrote to her, "There is nothing in me to attract a young girl's fancy, but my memory tells me that those who have known me very well have loved me very much."

Yet he seems not to have been at all confident of the answer he would get from Marie. He pleaded with her, "All that I ask, Mademoiselle, is that you will not be hasty in your judgment of me. You might make a mistake. Time will show you that, under a cold and shy outside, which doubtless displeases you, there is a heart full of affection for you."

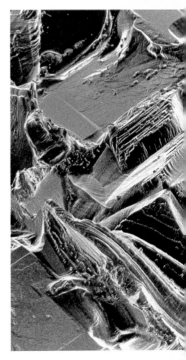

Sea salt crystals magnified by electron microscope. Developed in the 1930s, this instrument can produce images of structures up to a million times smaller than the eye can detect. Researchers were using it in the 1940s, when they first saw viruses.

"I woke up every morning with the thought that you wouldn't return my love, and then I wept! My work means nothing to me — to me, who was so devoted to my crystals that when I went to bed I wished the night was not so long, so that I could get back to work quicker!"
Louis, in a letter to Marie Laurent before their marriage

They were married on May 29, 1849. From the beginning Marie seems to have accepted Louis' overwhelming absorption in his work and to have grown used to a husband whose mind teemed with the events of his laboratory. She supported him, helped him, freed him from household cares, and allowed him complete freedom to do his research.

But she was more than a homemaker. Emile Roux, one of Pasteur's coworkers who later became famous for his own work, tells how she discussed his work, spurred his thinking on, and was therefore one of the best of his scientific collaborators.

So Louis settled into married life, and for the next five years they lived in Strasbourg. Louis was absorbed with his crystals and his teaching. Marie added to her role as wife and collaborator the demands of a mother, for in Strasbourg three of their five children were born: daughter Jeanne, followed a year later by a son, Jean-Baptiste, and two years later, baby Cécile.

To Lille, as professor of chemistry

September of 1854 brought a new challenge! Louis was made professor of chemistry and dean of the new Faculty of Sciences in Lille, a prosperous industrial city in the north of France where a great many gentlemen were in the trade of fermenting beetroot juice to make alcohol.

Louis was not quite thirty-two and very young for a position of such responsibility. It was an outstanding achievement. He took his teaching seriously. He wanted to infuse his students with the same sense of awe in the infinite realm of nature's miracles that he felt. "Has anybody a son," he exhorted a gathering of prosperous manufacturers and their wives, "who would not be interested if you gave him a potato and told him 'from that potato you can make sugar, from sugar you can make alcohol, from alcohol vinegar'?"

The students of Lille were interested. Louis Pasteur's lectures were events not to be missed. He swept his pupils off on energetic tours of the factories and foundries, the steel and metal works of France and Belgium.

The problem of the spoiled alcohol

Then came the day in 1856 when Monsieur Bigo asked for his advice. Monsieur Bigo was one of those manufacturers of alcohol from beet sugar and also the father of one of Louis' pupils. And he had a problem. Most of the time the process of changing beet-juice sugar into alcohol in his factory was going well. But in some of the vats the juice wasn't turning into alcohol; it was just turning sour. The spoiled vats were costing Monsieur Bigo thousands of francs a day.

Louis didn't know anything about alcohol manufacture and fermentation. He'd had some thoughts on fermentation, for his studies revolved around crystals found in wine barrels during fermentation. But no one really knew anything much about it except that it happened, and they had known that for thousands of years. You could take various crops, let them ferment, and turn them into alcoholic drinks like wine and beer. But no one knew what caused this.

Monsieur Bigo hoped that a man of science like his son's teacher might have some new suggestion. So Louis went along to the factory to have a look. He sniffed at the vats of fermenting sugar-beet juice. Here were the ones where the juice was turning to alcohol.

But here it was a very different matter. In these vats there was a slimy sour mess! Louis peered at it but was none the wiser. He decided he'd better have a closer look, properly, in his laboratory. So he put some of the sour stuff into bottles and, like the careful scientist he was, also took some of the good stuff. Then off he went.

Under the microscope

Under his microscope went a drop of liquid from a good vat. Why was he looking so intently? He didn't really know. Perhaps some familiar crystals would start him on a track to understanding this fermentation process or perhaps the well-trained scientist in him simply said it was best to have a good, long, hard, considered look before doing anything else.

At once, with the magnifying power of the microscope, he saw that the tiny drop of liquid was

"Pasteur was not a trained naturalist and he was working alone, without a tradition behind him and without associates with whom he could have shared his thoughts in moments of doubts or astonishment."

René Dubos,
Louis Pasteur:
Free Lance of Science

Large numbers of people worked in France's wine industry, like the workers in the vineyard pictured below. A great proportion of the harvest would often be lost in spoiled fermentation. Louis invented pasteurization to ensure a good product. (Painting by Edouard Debat-Ponsan)

filled with minute globules, little yellowish round and oval shapes that swarmed with darker specks. They were far smaller than any crystal he had ever seen! He searched his memory for some clue as to what they were. Then from one of those little corners of his mind, he dragged forth the realization that these must be the yeast cells that scientists knew were always in the mixture when sugar-beet juice or grapes were fermenting.

Scientists knew they were there. But they did not agree what they were doing there. There were several ideas. Some believed the yeast cells were a substance that was rotting and splitting the sugar molecules in sugar-beet or grape juice into alcohol and the clear gas called carbon dioxide.

The yeast was alive!

But the more Louis watched, the more he became convinced, with a mounting excitement, that the yeast globules were both alive and somehow at the bottom of this fermentation process — they were doing it!

He also remembered some German scientists who thought the yeasts were alive, and a scientist named Charles Cagniard de la Tour in France, who had poked around in breweries and reported seeing little buds on the yeasts.

Louis peered through his microscope again. Yes! He could see the buds. Hour after hour he watched, utterly absorbed in this miniature world. Then first one, then another bud grew larger and then split away, and there were three yeast globules where there had been only one.

He'd actually seen it! And it dawned on him that he also understood what was happening. The yeast globules were growing and multiplying, and as they did so they were feeding on the beet-juice sugar, turning it into alcohol and carbon dioxide!

But this still didn't solve his problem, Monsieur Bigo's problem: Why were some of the vats spoiled? He went back to work. A drop of the slimy stuff went under the microscope. No nice round globules of yeast here. He looked harder. None. He picked up the bottle and had a good look at it. There were specks stuck to the inside and floating in the liquid.

"Chance has frequently attended the birth of discovery. Chance evidence comes to everybody.... Without adequate scientific training, even the most intelligent individual remains incapable of interpreting the play of accidental factors, and incapable of experimentally reproducing some phenomena which chance has thrown in his way....
Hilaire Cuny,
Louis Pasteur:
The Man and His Theories

Opposite: Louis Pasteur in his laboratory.

27

The black rods

Were there any to be seen in the healthy stuff? He checked. No. Carefully, with some difficulty, he managed to get one of the specks into a drop of pure water and then to insert it under his microscope. He stared in disbelief.

Tiny black rods — millions and millions of minute rods in this single drop of water. They were busy in some kind of weird, shimmering dance that never stopped. They were much smaller than yeast. He tried to work out how big each was. They were unbelievably tiny. Each one could not be more than 1/25,000 of an inch (0.001 mm) long!

More hours went by as Louis, like Leeuwenhoek and Spallanzani before him, fell under the spell of these creatures. Back to the factory, he thought, quick! Nothing else mattered now except to follow his explorer's nose after these dancing rods.

He felt that he needed to observe more samples. Yes, just as he thought! The sourer the fermentation had become, the more of these creatures were in it.

And Pasteur began to understand clearly what was happening. These creatures had overrun the yeast

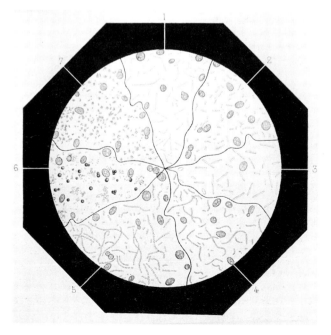

This sketch by Louis Pasteur is from his Studies on Beer, *published in 1876. It shows microorganisms that cause fermentation in various liquids, including spoiled wine, vinegar, and sour milk.*

cells. They had prevented them from making alcohol. Instead, these little rodlike things were manufacturing lactic acid, the same substance that makes milk sour.

But his instincts as a scientist did not falter. Don't jump to conclusions, he thought. Be sure. So it was back to the beet factory again. Examine more samples. Were there rods? Yes! It was clear. Always, when the vats had turned sour, the rods were there. And when they were there, there was no alcohol, only the acid of sour milk.

The alcohol industry is saved

He couldn't say how they got into the vats and he couldn't say from where. But even as early as this period in his work on microbes, he had a strong suspicion it was from the air.

He was able, however, to discuss with Monsieur Bigo how to be sure he would get good alcohol. He must test the liquid from the vats under a microscope. If he could see only the yeast cells, all would be well. But if even one of the rodlike creatures had made an appearance, he must throw it all away. He must destroy every bit of it. Once into the juice, the black rods would multiply into millions and wipe out the yeast cells.

To the alcohol manufacturers of Lille, Louis was a hero. Their industry was saved from ruin. Many, many families must have thanked Louis in heartfelt gratitude that year of 1856. In the pages of history, however, the world would eventually be grateful to Pasteur for much more.

But this experience in Bigo's sugar-beet factory had set Pasteur's feet on a track from which he would never be shaken.

He couldn't put these creatures out of his mind. He was certain that the rods caused the sour-milk acid. He was certain that the yeasts caused the alcohol. A picture became clearer and clearer in his mind, a picture of rods and yeast cells doing battle with one another.

It was a picture that was not to leave him for some time. It inspired him and drove him onward in his work on the microbes of disease.

Louis used this apparatus in his beer experiments. The left flask contained the wort, the ingredients from which beer is made. The wort was boiled to kill any microbes. The right flask contained a yeast culture. Air could enter through the curved glass tube on the right. Eighteen months later the beer in the left flask was still good because no microbes could travel up the curved tube.

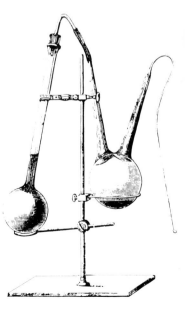

The equipment Pasteur used to pasteurize beer. The scientists of his day made most of their own equipment. Their laboratories were often unused cellars and attics.

Microbes

He couldn't study the rods properly, all tangled up in the pulp of sugar beets. So his first task was to find something they would grow in, something in which he could see them clearly.

He tried sugar first, mixed with water, for he knew there was always sugar in fermenting liquid. It was no good. They were very particular in their tastes, these dancing rods! He turned himself into a scientific cook. He painstakingly tried all sorts of mixtures — heating and filtering, then sowing his rods, and finding, with disappointment, that they did not grow.

But what about a broth made with yeast? He tried it. He put dried yeast into water. Then he added a little sugar, carefully measured. Next, he boiled it so that it would be completely free of any microbes, for he knew these microbes would be killed by heat. He strained the broth until it was perfectly clear. He wanted nothing to prevent him from watching the little rods.

Now, would the rods taken from the sick fermentations in Bigo's factory grow if they were left in this clear, germ-free yeast broth? He put a speck from a sick fermentation into a flask of the broth. Then he carefully carried the flask to his incubating oven, where the mixture could be kept comfortably warm as he observed it.

An anxious day passed, filled with a thousand other tasks for this busy teacher, for Pasteur also played an important role in the lives of the manufacturers and farmers of Lille. They frequently sought his advice and relied heavily on his opinions about manures and fertilizers.

Throughout the day, he kept his eye on his incubator. But whenever he peeped into it, nothing was happening. He almost became discouraged, yet he was certain, so very certain his guess was right.

His vigil at the incubator stretched from one day into two.

And then, at the end of what seemed an interminable second day, he saw something — bubbles, little bubbles of gas curling up through the broth. He squinted in the half-light, hardly daring to

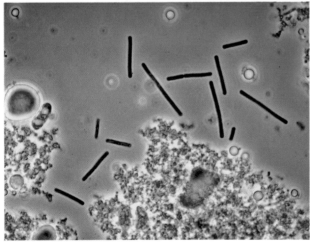

Above: Modern
pasteurization of wine
in stainless steel tanks
controlled by computers
in a German wine-
making company.

Left: A bacillus used to
produce yogurt from milk.
This is one of several kinds
of microbes that produce
lactic acid.

hope. They were coming from the speck he had sown! And surely there were specks that hadn't been there yesterday!

Black rods, by the millions

Under the microscope went a drop of the liquid, and he stared in sheer ecstasy! Millions of rods! The speck had spawned others. And — he checked, meticulously careful — yes, the same acid had appeared in his yeast broth, the acid of sour milk.

But he must be careful! There must be no jumping to conclusions. He needed absolute proof!

So he took some yeast broth containing rods and put it in more yeast broth, freshly boiled and free of germs. He waited again. The same thing happened. Each rod grew longer and longer and then split and became two rods where there had been one.

He put some in fresh milk. The milk soured and the rods multiplied. He did it again and then again, until he was certain beyond any doubt. If he added a tiny drop of rods to a clear broth, millions of new rods always appeared — and they always made the acid of sour milk.

The mystery is solved

He had solved the mystery of fermentation, the mystery that had remained unexplained for ten thousand years! These minute creatures were the cause of the fermentation. Just as yeast was the cause of the fermentation that changed sugar into alcohol, so these rods were the cause of the fermentation that produced lactic acid.

When he was absolutely certain, by August of 1857, he told everyone about it. He read a paper about it to the Lille Scientific Society. He told his students that fermentation was a living process caused by microscopic living creatures performing a giant's work. The students were enthralled. He wrote to his old teacher, Dumas, and prepared a statement for the Academy of Sciences in Paris, the pinnacle of scientific society in France, where reports on science throughout the world were read and discussed.

There was much excitement. Louis' conclusions flew in the face of the theories of several of the most

"To believe one has discovered an important scientific fact, to long to announce it, and yet to restrain oneself for days, weeks, sometimes even years; to strive to disprove one's own experiments; to publish one's discovery only after exhausting every alternative possibility — yes, the task is a hard one. But when . . . certainty is reached, the reward is one of the keenest joys of which the human soul is capable."
Louis Pasteur

respected scientists. They believed that fermentation was no more than a chemical reaction between substances when they were added together. We now know they were partially right. It is a substance produced by the yeast that causes alcoholic fermentation through a chemical reaction.

But how much more right was Louis, insisting that without yeast, a living organism, no alcoholic fermentation would take place!

Louis' work on fermentation went on for many years. He showed that microbes cause fermentation in many different substances. He also developed ways of preventing wine, vinegar, and beer from spoiling by killing harmful microbes with heat. This is the process named after him: pasteurization. Today every glass of pasteurized milk or yogurt, healthful and free of germs, is a testimony to Louis Pasteur.

Foreseeing the germ theory

His studies on fermentation convinced Louis that microbes were at the root of a host of other useful tasks in the world and at the heart of a thousand dangerous things too. Some day, some day he would prove it.

At the end of 1857, a new era had begun in his life. He was called back to his old school, the École Normale in Paris, to become Administrator and Director of Scientific Studies.

It was now that Louis came up against that old idea. It had lain in wait for him for a century since Spallanzani's efforts to finish it off. It was the theory of spontaneous generation.

Scientists no longer believed that humans, animals, or insects were produced except by parents of their own kind. But many believed that among microbes — fungi, yeasts, and other microorganisms — spontaneous generation did happen.

Everything in his fermentation work led Louis to the belief that microbes are already in the air and that we only notice them, with a microscope, when they land on solid matter or dive into liquids. He was not alone in believing this. Others, like his old teacher Dumas and Biot, rejected spontaneous generation.

But Louis Pasteur was never happy unless he had

A microscopic view of a wine bottle cork. Wine yeast can be seen as tiny balls against the cells of the cork.

"Nothing is more agreeable to a man who has made science his career than to increase the number of discoveries, but his cup of joy is full when the result of his observations is put to immediate practical use."
Louis Pasteur

33

proven something beyond a doubt. As an old man, he would say, "If I had to live my life over again, I would try always to remember that admirable precept of Bossuet: 'The greatest disorder of the mind is to believe that things are so because we wish them to be so.'"

On the brink of the most decisive conviction of his career, he knew there was only one way to go on. Proof and only proof would shift scientists in the direction he believed they must go.

Fermentation and putrefaction, or rotting, never took place unless microbes were present. That much he had proved. But it was generally believed that the microbes in, for example, corpses and rotten meat were caused by the rotting. No one saw it the other way around, that the microbes themselves caused the rotting. Yet everything in Louis' research pointed to that conclusion. But how to prove it?

Above: Fashionable Paris at the time of Louis Pasteur. He took walks in the city to relax from his long hours in the laboratory.

Left: The gatehouse of the École Normale, where Louis had his laboratory after he was appointed director of scientific studies. The cramped quarters were an improvement over his former laboratory in two attic rooms in another building of the school.

Professor Jean-Baptisté Biot, Louis' mentor and one of his long-standing supporters.

"If it is terrifying to think that life may be at the mercy of multiplication of those infinitesimally small creatures, it is also consoling to hope that Science will not always remain powerless before such enemies, since it is already now able to inform us that the simple contact of the air is sometimes enough to destroy them."

Louis Pasteur

The quest for proof

First he must find a way to show that microbes get into things from the outside. He must kill all the microbes in a sealed container and show that no new ones appeared.

So Louis set about devising an experiment very like Spallanzani's all those years before. He filled glass flasks with sugary yeast broth and boiled each flask to kill any microbes in it. While it boiled, he sealed it by melting the glass at the tip of the neck.

Then he divided the sealed flasks into two groups. He snapped off the tip of the necks of one group with pincers and allowed air in. Then he sealed them again by melting the glass. All the flasks in the second group he kept sealed. Then he put both groups in his incubating oven to keep them warm enough for any microbes to grow.

The results were unmistakable. In the flasks he had opened and then resealed, yeasts and other fungi were growing. In the flasks he had left sealed, nothing grew. Then he did it all over again. Then again and again and again — with flasks of milk, urine, and blood. He heated, he sealed, he opened, and he incubated them — just to test his idea as thoroughly as possible.

He had proved that germs came only from the outside. But those people who believed in spontaneous generation retaliated. His cutting off the air, they insisted to Pasteur, stopped the spontaneous generation; the microbes needed natural unheated air to burst into spontaneous life!

Louis gave a patient and restrained reply in return. "In my opinion, the question is wholly undecided. It is virgin territory and awaits the application of decisive proofs. What is there in the air that gives rise to these creatures? Are they germs? Or a solid substance? Or a fluid? Or a gas? All this is unknown, and we have to experiment to find the answers."

The final proof

And while his opponents pronounced on the subject, Pasteur went on to devise just such an experiment. He was convinced that it was not the air itself, but the dusts in the air that carried the microbes. But try as he might, he couldn't find a way to let air into his flasks without also letting microbes in.

Pasteur was rescued by Professor Antoine-Jérôme Balard, an elderly chemistry professor who liked to wander around the laboratories, having a look at others' work.

One day he strolled into Louis' laboratory and found him wrestling with his predicament. Like Biot, Dumas, and others, Professor Balard agreed with Louis about germs and air and thought it would be a fine thing to prove it. So he put his chemist's brain to the problem of Louis' flasks and his dustless air and came up with the solution.

Prepare the flasks, he told Pasteur, then heat and bend the necks in a long downward S-shape. Air would be able to pass through the necks, but dust would fall downward with the force of gravity. It would not be able to travel around the bends.

Excitedly Louis did this. Again he prepared his yeast broth and boiled it. As the liquid boiled, the air was forced out. But this time, as the liquid cooled, the air was drawn in while the dust and the microbes stuck in the long curving neck. The flasks remained clear, without contamination by microbes. Yet when he shook some so that the clear yeast broth flooded into the swan-necks, picking up the dust, then going back into the belly of the flask, they became filled with microbes, multiplying gleefully!

Even today, over a century later, the swan-necked flasks remain clear, still proving the simple truth of Louis' experiment. They are also important reminders of the simple generosity of scientists like Professor Balard, a person who shared his insights so the truth might emerge.

The search for pure air again

Louis reasoned that the amount of dust in the air would vary in different places. Surely there would be more dust in a busy street in Paris than there would be at the top of a mountain?

So, he decided, his next task must be to show that there were different amounts of microbes in the air in these different places. He must move out of the laboratory into the world.

"There is here no question of religion, philosophy, atheism, materialism, or spiritualism. I might even add they do not matter to me as a scientist. It is a question of fact; when I took it up, I was as ready to be convinced by experiments that spontaneous generation exists as I am now persuaded that those who believe it are blindfolded."
                                    Louis Pasteur

By now he had assistants helping him. Together, they prepared sealed flasks of yeast broth. They carried ten to the cellars of the Paris Observatory, eleven more to the yard of the observatory, twenty up a hill near Louis' hometown of Arbois, and twenty more up Mont Blanc.

Of the ten flasks opened in the cellars, only one developed microbes. This, Louis suggested, was because the air was still, so there would be little dust. In the yard, however, eleven out of eleven went bad. On the hill near Arbois, only eight out of twenty grew microbes, and on another, higher hill, only five out of twenty. And out of the twenty flasks taken up Mont Blanc, only one developed microbes.

In November 1860, Louis reported the results of his experiment to the Academy of Sciences: "They enable us, in my opinion, to state definitely that the dusts suspended in the atmosphere are the exclusive origin, the initial, indispensable condition for the existence of life in the liquids."

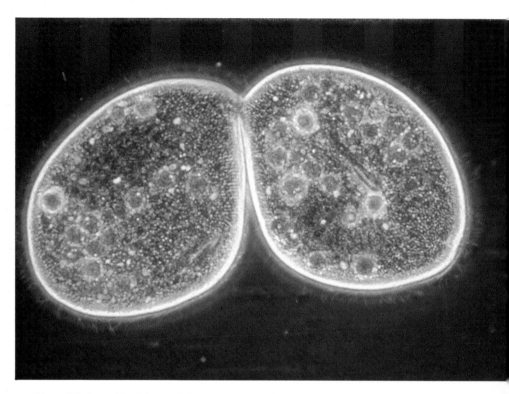

He added, with his unfailing sense of vision, "What would be most desirable of all would be to carry these studies far enough to prepare the way for serious research into the origin of different diseases."

A microscopic protozoan in the final stages of division into two organisms. Like other scientists before him, Pasteur observed that many microbes increase by dividing.

Years of dedication

And so Louis Pasteur had launched himself and the scientists of his time on this voyage of discovery. He did his experiments, these and a thousand others, all with the same clarity and persistence.

Over the next ten years, while the argument continued, often quite bitterly, he systematically demolished all the objections of his opponents. There was much opposition to him. Some of it was on scientific grounds, but some was because several firmly established scientists wished to oppose this confident young man who blasted into their midst with the air of being right from the top of his head to the tip of his toes.

But Louis responded to his opponents in the best

"The whole secret of Pasteur's success may be summed up in a few words. It consisted in the application of the exact methods of physical and chemical research to problems which had hitherto been attacked by other less precise and less systematic methods."
Sir Henry Roscoe, The Life Work of a Chemist

Below, top: Louis and his wife in 1889. Madame Pasteur devoted herself to Louis and his work.

Below, bottom: Louis, with his granddaughter. Family life meant a great deal to him.

way a scientist can. He performed his meticulous experiment in public for the Academy of Sciences — and was seen to be right.

In 1862, when he was nearly forty, Pasteur was elected to the Academy. His life was now filled with lectures that fired the imagination of his fellow scientists. So many of his colleagues and students were ripe for this prophet in their midst. So many were eager to grasp the weapons of understanding he handed them.

These were exciting years — these years of the 1850s and 1860s — for science and for the world! But quietly, in Louis' private life, these were also years of bitter tragedy. In September of 1859, his eldest daughter, Jeanne, became ill and died suddenly from typhoid fever. She was only nine years old. We are not told much about the events that surround this tragedy in the Pasteur family. But who knows what deep core of determination may have grown from this loss and helped to propel this extraordinary scientist forward in his crusade to find ways that we might control disease?

Germs, germs everywhere

Pasteur decided that the world at large must learn about germs. So April of 1864 found him speaking at the university of the Sorbonne to a large audience made up of students, famous authors, scientists, and ministers of state. He plunged the hall into darkness. Then he shone a beam of light. He directed it across the room so that those assembled might see the millions of dust particles suspended in the air. He spoke to his spellbound listeners of the multitudes of germs drifting within these particles.

And he showed his two flasks, one with its yeast broth cloudy with microbes and the other with its yeast broth still clear, four years after he had performed the experiment. The broth, he pointed out, was still protected from the germs in the dust by the long curving neck of the flask.

"What is the difference between the two?" he asked his fascinated audience. "They are full of the same liquid, they are full of the same air, and they are both open. The only difference is this: in this one, the dust of the air and its germs can fall into the flask and reach the liquid and produce microscopic beings. In this other it is impossible, or very difficult, for the germs of the air to reach the liquid."

But Pasteur was not content merely to convert the world to the germ theory. He began acting as a wine doctor too. The winemakers of his hometown of Arbois requested his help. They were having problems. Some of their wine turned sour, like vinegar, and would not keep for any length of time.

Louis turned his microscope on the wine and peered. He discovered the culprits. There were microbes lurking in the vats. Some were making the wine sour, and others were making it bitter. Carefully he set up experiments, working with the wine. Finally, he was able to tell the winemakers exactly how to heat the wine, just after it had finished fermenting, in order to kill these microbes without damaging the wine itself. Pasteur had invented the process the world would call pasteurization.

"I cannot keep my thoughts from my poor little girl, so good, so happy in her little life who, in this fatal year now ending, was taken away from us."

Pasteur, writing to his father about Jeanne's death in 1859

Louis Pasteur at work in his laboratory at the École Normale, as shown in this 1884 engraving from the French science magazine La Nature.

The germ theory is applied

In Scotland a far-sighted doctor by the name of Joseph Lister, who was a professor of surgery in Edinburgh, read about Pasteur's proof of germs in the air. Here was what he had been searching for in the struggle to control infection in hospitals. Experimenting swiftly with ways of killing germs, Lister brought about a transformation that was little short of a miracle.

At this time, hospitals were grim places, stinking with the smell of blood and pus-filled wounds. More often than not, people died not from the illnesses they had come into the hospital with, but from infections they developed once there. The death rate after operations was very high. Many of Lister's patients seemed to be getting better, but on about the fourth day, they would develop an infection in the wound and die not long after.

But by 1867, in Lister's wards, all the instruments and equipment used to dress wounds were dipped in a strong solution of carbolic acid. This would destroy germs. Medical workers scrubbed their hands with

43

Scottish surgeon Joseph Lister, who introduced antiseptic methods into his surgery. This reduced fatalities to about three out of a hundred.

carbolic acid. A carbolic acid spray played on the wound during the operation. Later the wound was washed with carbolic solution, and Lister used antiseptic materials for dressings.

At one time, at least fifty out of every hundred patients died after operations. Even in the early trials of his new methods, Lister reduced the death rate to fifteen out of every hundred, and then to three out of every hundred. He was thrilled with his success in reducing the death rate and grateful for Pasteur's work with germs.

Years later, in 1874, he wrote a letter to Louis Pasteur. "Allow me," Lister said, "to take this opportunity to tender you my most cordial thanks for having, by your brilliant researches, demonstrated to me the truth of the germ theory of putrefaction . . . furnishing me with the principles upon which alone the antiseptic system can be carried out."

The change in the use of antiseptics began later in France. After the Franco-Prussian War of 1870-71, a surgeon began considering Pasteur's ideas. He began to wonder if germs were the cause of the stinking decay that was settling into the soldiers' wounds. Persuaded by the work of Pasteur and Lister, he began disinfecting surgical instruments and filtering the air around wounds.

The germ theory of disease, again

But the question of what caused disease in the body as a whole remained open. Scientists continued to conjecture. Most doctors believed that disease was somehow in the body; it was "in us and of us and brought into being by us."

But the idea that disease and rotting were connected was also an old one. Two hundred years before Pasteur, the English scientist Robert Boyle said, "He that thoroughly understands the nature of ferments and fermentations, shall probably be much better able than he that ignores them, to give a fair account of diverse phenomena of several diseases."

Now Louis, this man who understood ferments, was pushed by an unexpected combination of circumstances to take his first steps along the path that opened those floodgates of knowledge.

Modern silkworms are raised under antiseptic conditions to prevent disease. Pasteur taught the growers how to examine the eggs for microbes and established the importance of cleanliness.

Above: A silkworm moth among silk chrysalises. The moth lays up to four hundred eggs at a time. The silkworms hatch out ten days later.

Upper left: Silkworms feeding on mulberry leaves. When about six weeks old, the silkworm spins a cocoon around itself composed of a single silk strand 3,000 feet (1,000 m) or more long.

Lower left: A cocoon cut away to show the chrysalis inside. Some chrysalises are allowed the two weeks in the cocoon to develop into mature moths. But most are destroyed by heat and the silk thread is unwound from the cocoon.

Opposite: Hundreds of people in Paris died each day in the cholera epidemic of 1865. Pasteur and others failed to discover if the disease was caused by a microbe. But Robert Koch found the cholera microbe and proved that it was spread through contaminated drinking water.

So Louis saved the people of the silkworm lands who depended on these little creatures' spinning their silken cocoons. He had learned how vital it was to be unfailingly methodical and complete in his work. He had also found out that healthy worms became sick when the droppings from sick worms soiled the mulberry leaves they ate. The second disease that had confused him, called *flacherie*, was passed on through the intestines of the worms. In effect, he had showed the importance of the environment in spreading disease.

Vital new ideas! Disease must have been very much on people's minds in those years. Cholera had broken out in Paris and Marseilles. In Paris alone, people were dying at the rate of two hundred a day.

Sorrow takes a crippling toll

Disease must have been on Louis' mind in a very personal way too. He had already lost his eldest daughter Jeanne, dead from typhoid fever. In September of 1865, the baby of the family, his two-year-old daughter, Camille, became ill and died.

Only a few months later Cécile, twelve years old, also caught typhoid fever. By May of 1866, she too was dead.

It took an appalling toll on Louis. There was the terrible frustration of seeing that the doctors could not save his children; there were the problems of his own work on the silkworms, and there was also the sense of responsibility to people who depended for their survival on his getting his conclusions right. In October of 1868, he was back in Paris. On the nineteenth he woke up feeling rather strange. All down his left side there was a tingling sensation.

By afternoon Pasteur was convulsed with shivering. But he had promised to present a paper to the Academy of Sciences that evening. It was to be on behalf of an Italian scientist and he felt he must go. When Pasteur came home, he went to bed, still feeling ill. During the night his condition worsened. He could no longer speak or move. The whole of his left side was paralyzed.

He was nearly forty-six, and he had had a stroke. They thought he was going to die.

Le Petit Journal

ADMINISTRATION
61, RUE LAFAYETTE, 61

Les manuscrits ne sont pas rendus

On s'abonne sans frais
dans tous les bureaux de poste

5 CENT.

SUPPLÉMENT ILLUSTRÉ

23ᵐᵉ Année

5 CENT.

Numéro 1.150

ABONNEMENTS

	SIX MOIS	UN AN
SEINE et SEINE-ET-OISE	2 fr.	3 fr. 50
DÉPARTEMENTS	2 fr.	4 fr. »
ÉTRANGER	2 60	5 fr. »

DIMANCHE 1ᵉʳ DÉCEMBRE 1912

LE CHOLÉRA

49

Louis Pasteur and some of his associates. He depended upon these men to carry out his experiments after a stroke in 1868 left him partially paralyzed.

Recovery

But Louis Pasteur would defy predictions. He managed to speak again, at first only single words, and then fluently. A week later, he was dictating notes to his assistants. Although he was paralyzed in the left arm and leg, he refused to let this problem stop him from working. Within three months, he was on his way to Alais to see how the silkworm research he had begun was progressing.

From this time on, he was not able to handle the scientific apparatus needed for the work by himself, so he became dependent on his assistants to perform the careful manipulations necessary for the experiments he devised. Many great scientists were to be born of these close partnerships with Louis Pasteur during this period. They were infected by his style, filled with his enthusiasm, inspired by his unfailing strength of spirit, and impressed by his integrity as a scientist.

The more he studied silkworms, the more certain Pasteur became that there was a link between the fermentations of yeasts and disease in animals and humans. Again he sounded his clarion call to his fellows: "It is in the power of man to make parasitic illnesses disappear from the face of the globe, if the doctrine of spontaneous generation is wrong, as I am sure it is."

Yet doctors as a body dismissed these predictions, despite the work being done and reports being made. Epidemic diseases, due just to a microbe! Nonsense! It was a country doctor in Germany who turned these predictions into fact and stopped for all time the doubts about the significance of what Louis Pasteur had shown.

One microbe, one disease

In East Prussia, in the heart of farm country, there was a man named Robert Koch. At one time, Koch had wanted to be an explorer, but he had become a doctor. And he was frustrated by his inability to do anything to cure disease.

But one year he was given a microscope for his birthday by his wife. She hoped it would help to quiet her husband's restlessness. One day Koch turned his microscope on some gluey black blood. This had been taken from animals that had died of anthrax, a disease that at this time was wiping out whole herds of sheep and cattle throughout Europe. At once, Koch noticed the familiar rodlike microbes swarming in the sick blood.

He followed his curious nose and his restless explorer's instinct with a thousand tests and experiments — and then a thousand more. In time, he proved that the rodlike things were alive. They multiplied, they were never found in healthy animals, and they were able to survive as spores, lurking until they could burst into activity again. The anthrax microbe, *Bacillus anthracis*, and it alone, caused the disease of anthrax.

In April of 1876, three years after he had started work on the problem, Koch went to see his old professors. He told them what he had seen in his examinations of the black blood. There it was: one microbe caused one disease. Pasteur had repeatedly said it and suggested it in the silkworm disease. Koch had proved it.

Now the hunt was on for the microbes that had been slaughtering people year after year throughout the world — and still were: cholera, typhoid, tuberculosis, pneumonia, syphilis, diphtheria, the Russian plague. In the decades that followed, all these were the focus of scientists' prying lenses as they tried to track down the microbes, grow them, and learn how they lived and died.

Koch had proved the cause and Pasteur now set his heart to search for the cure.

Robert Koch proved the principle that one microbe caused one specific disease. The four steps to establish this are today called Koch's postulates.

The dawn of immunology

Pasteur was becoming more and more convinced of his theories during these important years. With increasing clarity, he saw disease as a form of struggle for existence! There was a contest being waged between microbes and the tissues they continually tried to invade.

During his travels around France, he had seen a cow that had had anthrax but had recovered naturally from it. He had seen that later, when the cow was injected with powerful anthrax bacilli, it did not die!

"How I wish I had enough health and sufficient knowledge to throw myself body and soul into the experimental study of one of our infectious diseases."
    Louis Pasteur, in a letter,
    December 1873

The idea took root in his mind that having the disease somehow caused the body to develop a resistance against it. There the idea lurked, waiting for the right moment to blossom forth.

Louis was not a doctor, and there were many doctors who thought that laboratory scientists like him should not be meddling in medicine. But there were enough who recognized the impact that Pasteur's research was making, and in 1873 he was elected to the Academy of Medicine.

He took on some young assistants: Dr. Jules-Francois Joubert, Dr. Emile Roux, and Dr. Charles Chamberland. They brought their expertise in chemistry, physics, and bacteriology to Pasteur's laboratory. More and more, Pasteur's work turned to the search for control of disease-causing microbes.

Chance — and the greatest breakthrough

In 1878 he began studying the microbe that caused a poultry disease called chicken cholera. It had recently killed a tenth of the chickens in France. Pasteur was growing the microbes in chicken broth and had seen that when injected into chickens, the broth culture killed them within days.

It was summertime. Louis and his assistants went on vacation, and a culture of chicken cholera microbes was put to one side and forgotten. On returning, Louis was about to throw it away when he changed his mind and decided to inject it into a hen.

In went a syringeful. The hen became mildly sick but recovered quickly. By the time hens usually showed signs of the disease, she was still well! And in the days that followed she stayed well, happily strutting around her cage.

Greatly excited — for he remembered the cow that had not died of anthrax — Louis injected more hens with the old culture. They joined the first in strutting around the cages. His brain aflame with what he dared to hope was happening, he injected them with a fresh culture, strong enough to kill. Each hen got the fatal dose.

They were unaffected. He injected the fresh culture into another batch of hens, one that had not been inoculated with the old culture. They all died.

Opposite, top: Anthrax bacteria, Bacillus anthracis, in a false-color electron micrograph. Anthrax can cause the death of animals and humans within hours of infection.

Opposite, below: Bacillus anthracis rods in animal tissue. In humans, the disease attacks the lungs or the skin. People can catch the disease from infected animals or improperly prepared hides and furs.

"In the field of experimentation chance favors the prepared mind," Louis once said. He understood immediately what this all meant. An English doctor named Edward Jenner had used the microbes of the mild disease of cowpox to vaccinate against smallpox, and this was now widely done in Europe.

But Jenner's methods were based on using a disease known to be harmless to people to produce protection against a disease that was dangerous.

What was happening with chicken cholera was different. Weakened microbes of the disease itself had raised the hen's own defenses so she could fight off the disease.

Could it be done again? His mind buzzed with the problems. And one by one, by experimenting, he answered all the questions. He decided to call the treatment vaccination after Jenner's method. And we still use the term now for this technique of immunization, preventing a disease by inoculating in advance against it.

How many other microbes could be grown in the laboratory, weakened, and used as vaccines? What excitement he must have felt!

For so long he had called for this and worked for it. The rest of his life would be devoted to a laborious search for ways of weakening microbes' ability to multiply, weakening them enough not to cause the disease but enough to force the body's natural defenses to arm themselves.

The anthrax vaccine

For some time, Louis had also been studying the disease of anthrax, the disease on which Koch had already done such magnificent work. Scientists knew what caused it, but still the cattle-rearing provinces of France were losing thousands of cattle each year. Sheep flocks were devastated; sometimes as many as half died. People also died from it; a scratch was enough to kill.

The search for an anthrax vaccine took many years. Pasteur and his team started work on anthrax in 1877; in 1879 they made the discovery of chicken cholera. Not until February of 1881 did Louis believe they had succeeded with anthrax vaccine.

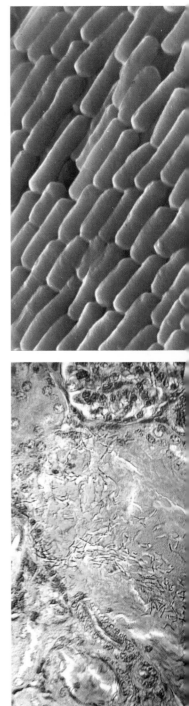

A doctor inoculating sheep against anthrax by the Pasteur method.

The great challenge

He accepted a challenge from farmers in Melun, near Paris, to test it in public. It is famous, that day in May 1881, at the farm of Pouilly-le-Fort. Animal doctors and farmers, ministers of state, scientists, and reporters gathered to see Louis and his assistants, Roux, Chamberland, and Louis Thuillier — and the sheep.

Twenty-five sheep received two vaccinations with weakened microbes; first with very old, weak ones, then twelve days later with fresher, stronger ones to build up their resistance. Another twenty-five sheep received no vaccinations at all. The two groups were kept in separate fields. Finally, all fifty were given fatal doses of powerful anthrax microbes.

Publicly confident, Louis was privately consumed with worry, unable to sleep and unable to open the telegram from Pouilly-le-Fort telling the results. Madame Pasteur had to open it for him, but her own hands were also trembling.

Government officials, scientists, and farmers gathered, buzzing while the numbers were counted

"The general principles have been found and one cannot refuse to believe that the future is rich with the greatest hopes."

Pasteur, speaking of the anthrax vaccine

and counted again. All the vaccinated sheep were healthy. All the unvaccinated were dead or dying. Success! What a roar of cheers greeted Pasteur and his fellow workers as they arrived at Melun!

Within no time, Pasteur's laboratories were turned over to making the vaccine. And the tireless Roux, Chamberland, and Thuillier rushed across France, injecting animals until they saw injection syringes in their sleep. In under a year, thousands of animals were vaccinated. By 1894, some 3,400,000 sheep and 438,000 head of cattle had also been vaccinated.

There were problems with the vaccine. They had difficulty making it pure enough. Sometimes it caused anthrax. Sometimes it just didn't work. The giant leap in medical knowledge was undeniable. A vaccine had been prepared that could prevent, in advance, a disease that had been devastating farming areas throughout Europe.

His final crusade

Today, many people remember Pasteur more for curing rabies than for curing anthrax. Rabies was a terrible disease. A bite from a rabid dog or wolf could infect persons. They would begin to shake, would feel as though they were being strangled, and either die from suffocation or be paralyzed.

Because people infected with rabies always went into convulsions, Louis and his team reasoned that the microbe was probably in the central nervous system, in the brain and spinal cord.

So they took nerve tissue, fragments from the spinal cord of a dog that had died from rabies, and injected it into a rabbit. Two weeks later the rabbit had rabies. They took some of its spinal cord when it died and injected it into another rabbit; and so on, until it had been transferred twenty-five times. And the time for the disease to develop had become shorter, until it was only a week. Then they took a fragment of infected spinal marrow and looked for ways of weakening it.

In March of 1885 Louis wrote to a friend, "I have demonstrated this year that one can vaccinate dogs or render them immune to rabies. I have not dared to treat humans bitten by rabid dogs."

Pasteur experimenting with rabies in rabbits. He was unable to find a microbe responsible for rabies; today we know it is caused by a virus.

"Your father is as preoccupied as ever; he hardly speaks to me, sleeps little, and rises at dawn, in short, he is leading the same life as I began sharing with him, thirty-five years ago today."
Madame Pasteur, writing to her children on her wedding anniversary, 1884

A young shepherd, Jean-Baptiste Jupille, being inoculated against rabies. He was the second human treated with the new rabies vaccine.

The boy with rabies

One Monday morning, on July 6, 1885, nine-year-old Joseph Meister arrived at Pasteur's laboratory with his mother. He had been attacked in his village by a rabid dog that bit his hands, legs, and thighs.

But the vaccine wasn't ready for humans yet, so Pasteur asked the advice of colleagues from the Academy of Medicine: Would the boy develop rabies? Fourteen deep wounds? Yes! The vaccine might also kill him, but if not inoculated Joseph might die anyway or be completely paralyzed.

Louis decided to take the plunge. On the evening of July 6, he supervised a doctor injecting the extract from the weakened spinal cord of a rabbit that had died of rabies fifteen days before. Over the next ten days, they gave more injections, each day a stronger one. The bites healed; Joseph never contracted rabies.

The news of his cure flashed around the world. From all over Europe, people who had been bitten by rabid animals flooded into Paris for treatment. We will never know how many survived because of the

Above: Louis' rooms at the Pasteur Institute in Paris, where he spent most of his last years.

Left: This statue of Jean-Baptiste Jupille stands on the grounds of the Pasteur Institute in Paris. The fifteen-year-old shepherd was bitten by a rabid dog that he fought and killed in order to protect several children. His life was saved by Pasteur's rabies vaccine.

Dr. Emile Roux injecting a horse during his study of the toxins of diphtheria.

Elie Metchnikov worked to find the ways that the body develops immunity to microbes and overcomes infection.

vaccine, for rabies doesn't always kill its victims. But many of them would have died. The crucial jump had been made from animals to humans. The Academy of Sciences founded an institute, to be called the Pasteur Institute, for the treatment of rabies.

The world responded; money poured in.

Pasteur's final years

Louis continued working until he was nearly seventy. In 1887, when he was sixty-four, another paralytic stroke prevented him from personally doing experimental work. But his dialogue with pupils and collaborators never ceased. In November 1888, the Pasteur Institute officially opened, and he was able to see them continue in the spirit of enthusiasm and determination that had been the guiding impetus of his own life.

On September 28, 1895, when seventy-two, he died surrounded by family, colleagues, and students. For nearly half a century, he had dominated science. For a quarter of a century, he had labored despite partial paralysis of his body. Now the body was dead. But the spirit was not. It lived on in the scientists and doctors who inherited the knowledge he bequeathed.

Pasteur's legacy

The young men he had trained went on to new glories. Dr. Roux and Dr. Alexandre Yersin developed the treatment for diphtheria, a disease that once killed thousands of children every year. Elie Metchnikov, one of Pasteur's most brilliant assistants, would begin to lay bare the ways that the body develops a resistance to microbes and develops immunity.

Dr. Yersin discovered the microbe that causes the plague. When Pasteur, old and retired, had looked through the microscope at it, his only comment had been, "Ah, what a lot there is still to do!"

It is too easy to talk of Pasteur, the genius who did it all, and too easy to say that if he hadn't, someone else would have. Nothing is achieved by one person's effort; all is a part of the times in which people live and the accumulation of knowledge brought about by many, so that it is possible to draw together the strands and push forward the frontiers, as did Pasteur.

But there is also the man, and who knows what might have been if Pasteur had not been the fighter he was, with that fierce determination to bring about the changes he believed in? And what if other visionary scientists, like Joseph Lister, had not recognized the truth when they saw it and produced the revolution around Pasteur's work?

Pasteur had once said to his fellow scientists, "You bring me the deepest joy that can be felt by a man whose invincible belief it is that science and peace will triumph over ignorance and war . . . that the future will belong to those who will have done most for suffering humanity."

One wonders, thinking of Pasteur's enormous life, if his last words to Madame Pasteur as she offered him water — the words, "I can't" — perhaps signaled the first time he entertained the notion of failure.

Joseph Lister greets Louis Pasteur during the celebration of Pasteur's seventieth birthday at the Sorbonne. Pasteur is leaning on the arm of the president of the French Republic.

"You have raised the veil that for all the centuries made infectious illnesses a dark mystery."

Joseph Lister, to Pasteur, at his jubilee

The work continues

Events moved swiftly following Pasteur's pioneering work against microbial disease in the 1870s and 1880s. By the end of the century, most of the bacteria that caused common diseases had been identified, many of them in Pasteur's laboratory in France and in the laboratories of Robert Koch in Germany.

Even before Pasteur's death in 1895, the first evidence of a disease caused by a virus had accumulated, although it was not until the 1940s that viruses were first seen with an electron microscope.

The diphtheria toxin had been isolated by Roux and Yersin in 1888 at the Pasteur Institute. The tetanus toxin had been identified by scientists in Robert Koch's laboratory in 1890. Antidotes to these toxins soon followed.

In the twentieth century, effective vaccines have been developed against smallpox, tuberculosis, yellow fever, poliomyelitis, cholera, measles, typhoid, whooping cough, rubella, influenza, and bubonic plague.

The major leap of the twentieth century has been the development of the antibiotic drugs. After the first use of penicillin in 1941, other antibiotics were developed. This is a fitting culmination to the hundred years since Louis Pasteur's work on fermentation set scientists' feet on the march against disease.

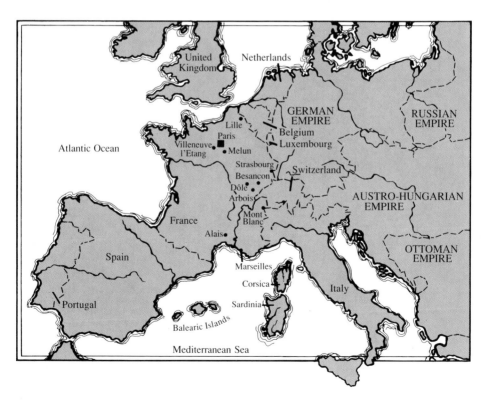

For More Information . . .

Organizations

The organizations listed below will provide you with more information about communicable diseases, public health, and other subjects pertaining to the natural sciences. When you write, be sure to explain what you want to know and remember to include your name, address, and age.

Young Scientists of America Foundation
P.O. Box 9066
Phoenix, AZ   85068

World Health Organization
Avenue Appia
CH-1211
Geneva 27, Switzerland

U.S. Center for Disease Control
1600 Clifton Road NE
Building 1, Room 2167
Atlanta, GA   30333

Books

The following books will help you learn more about Louis Pasteur, microbiology, communicable diseases, and other persons in the health field. Check your local library or bookstore to see if they have them or can order them for you.

About Louis Pasteur —

Louis Pasteur. Bains (Troll)
Louis Pasteur: Young Scientist. Sabin (Troll)

About Microbiology —

Bacteria: How They Affect Other Living Things. Patent (Holiday)
Microbes and Bacteria. Sabin (Troll)
Microscopic Animals and Plants. Patent (Holiday)
Viruses. Nourse (Franklin Watts)
Viruses: Life's Smallest Enemies. Knight (Morrow)

About Communicable Diseases —

Breakthrough: The True Story of Penicillin. Jacobs (Dodd)
Germs! Patent (Holiday)
Germs Make Me Sick: A Health Handbook for Kids.
    Donahue and Capellaro (Knopf)
Your Immune System. Nourse (Franklin Watts)

About Other Persons in the Health Field —

Great Women of Medicine. Hume (Random House)
Florence Nightingale. Brown (Gareth Stevens)

Magazines

Here are some magazines that feature articles on science, technology, and nature. Look for them in your library, or write to the addresses listed below for information about subscribing. Remember to include your name and address.

Current Science
245 Long Hill Road
Middletown, CT   06457

Science Challenge
3500 Western Avenue
Highland Park, IL   60035

National Geographic World
National Geographic Society
17th and M Streets NW
Washington, DC   20036

3-2-1 Contact
Children's Television Workshop
One Lincoln Plaza
New York, NY   10023

Science World
2931 East McCarty Street
Jefferson City, MO   65102

Glossary

Anthrax
A disease of cattle and sheep that can be passed on to humans very easily. Humans will experience fever and a swollen throat. It is caused by a bacillus and is almost always fatal, unless vaccine is immediately available. Pasteur developed a vaccine to be used on animals. Anthrax bacilli produce spores that can remain inactive for decades, but still produce living bacilli under the right conditions.

Bacillus (plural: **bacilli**)
A bacterium shaped like a rod. A bacterium shaped like a small round ball is called a *coccus* (plural: *cocci*). A bacterium shaped like a corkscrew is called a *spirochete*. The shape helps microbiologists identify the organism.

Bacterium (plural: **bacteria**)
Any one of a large group of simple organisms of one cell that multiply by splitting into two new organisms. They are so tiny they can be seen only with a microscope. Some of them cause disease. They are mostly responsible for the decay of dead plants and animals.

Carbolic acid
A poisonous, colorless acid used as an antiseptic and disinfectant.

Cholera
A serious illness of the intestines caused by drinking water containing the cholera microbe. It is passed on by human or animal feces. Humans experience severe diarrhea and stomach cramps. In the 1832 French epidemic, the death rate from this disease was twenty-three in every thousand people.

Chrysalis
The pupa of a butterfly or moth living in a case or cocoon. The pupa is the form of

the insect between the larval, or caterpillar, and adult stages. During this resting period, the insect changes into the adult form and then hatches out.

Cocoon

A covering that a butterfly or moth secretes around itself for protection during the chrysalis stage. The cocoon of the silkworm moth is the source of silk fiber that is made into clothing.

Crystal

A tiny fragment of a substance that has a definite, orderly structure. Its surface is made up of smooth faces, or facets, arranged in a pattern that reflects the internal atomic or molecular arrangement of the substance.

Culture

As a verb, this word means to grow microorganisms in a nutritious liquid or gelatinlike substance in conditions designed to help it develop. As a noun, it refers to the growth itself that results.

Diphtheria

A serious disease very easily passed on among humans. It is caused by a bacillus that produces a poison that is released into the person's bloodstream. Diphtheria often used to be fatal in small children. The infected child experienced a high fever and difficulty in breathing and swallowing. Eventually a skin formed inside the child's throat, blocking it completely; then the child choked to death.

Dissymmetry

The kind of likeness between two objects when one is the mirror image of the other. It is symmetry in opposite directions; a good example is a person's hands.

Fermentation

A process in which microorganisms break down the composition of plant or animal materials. Bacteria and yeasts especially are involved. Pasteur's work caused scientists to classify fermentation into types. The most important types are the following: *alcoholic*, in which alcohol is produced, as during wine or beer making; *acetic*, in which wine and other alcohols are turned into vinegar; and *lactic*, in which the sugars in milk are turned into acids, as, for example, when milk turns sour.

Germ

A disease-causing microorganism. In popular terminology, a microbe. The original meaning is a "bud" or "seed."

Immunize

To protect against a specific disease, usually by inoculation.

Incubator

An insulated box or oven that keeps its contents at a constant temperature.

Inoculate

To place a measured dose of a weakened bacillus or other disease-causing microbe into a human or animal in order to cause the body to produce its own defense against the disease. Also called vaccination.

Latin Quarter

An area of Paris on the south, or "left," bank of the Seine River where the university of the Sorbonne and other educational institutions are situated. In the nineteenth century, most students and artists lived there because of the cheap lodgings.

Lens

A polished piece of glass or other clear material in which one or both sides are curved; usually used to enlarge images of small things so that their details can be observed. Lenses are used in microscopes, telescopes, and similar instruments.

Maggot

The second, or larval, stage of flies. Maggots hatch out from eggs the adult fly has laid in rotting substances like meat. The maggots feed on the rotting matter.

Microbe

Another name for microorganism.

Microbiology

The study of microorganisms, especially bacteria and yeasts.

Microorganism

A living thing made of a single cell and too small to be seen with the naked eye. Bacteria, yeasts, and viruses are microorganisms.

Pasteurization

A process, pioneered by Pasteur, of heating wine, beer, and similar products to prevent harmful bacteria from ruining the fermentation. Also used on milk and other foods to destroy harmful bacteria. Tuberculosis was a common disease among humans until the practice of pasteurizing milk became widespread.

Plague

A disease caused by a bacillus and spread by fleas from infected rats. In the 1300s, the bubonic plague, or the Black Death, killed up to half the population of Europe.

Pneumonia

An infection of the lungs. The lungs partly fill with fluid and the flooded areas cannot be used for breathing. It is caused by a virus or by various types of bacteria.

Rabies

A disease of the nervous system of warm-blooded animals caused by a virus. It is passed on to humans by the bite of an infected animal. Infected creatures and humans experience a heavy flow of saliva and convulsions. Humans also develop throat spasms that prevent them from drinking water. From this came its other name, hydrophobia, from the Greek words meaning "water" and "fear of." Before Pasteur developed his vaccine, death was the usual result of a rabid animal's bite.

Smallpox

An easily spread disease of humans caused by a virus. Infected persons experience a high fever and a rash that causes scabs to form. When the scabs fall off, they leave permanent pits in the skin. In 1796 Dr. Edward Jenner pioneered vaccination against this disease. Although not always fatal, it was a major killer until well into the twentieth century. It is now considered eradicated from the world.

Solution

One or more gaseous, liquid, or solid substances dissolved in another substance, most commonly a liquid. The molecules of the substance or substances are spread evenly throughout the liquid.

Spontaneous generation

An old scientific theory that, under the right conditions, life would appear without any cause. Maggots were often given as an example because people did not realize that they were the result of flies laying their eggs on a rotting substance. Pasteur proved that this theory was wrong and that life always comes from other life.

Spore

Any small body, usually of a single cell, that can give rise to a new adult organism. Spores are often produced by certain types of bacteria and other microorganisms. Some spores develop into the adult form immediately. Other spores can stay in a resting state for years or decades before developing into adults.

Stereochemistry

A branch of chemistry that studies how atoms of a molecule are arranged in space; a study of the ways that these arrangements control how chemicals react. Pasteur's discovery of dissymmetry in crystals gave rise to this new science.

Stroke

The popular name for the blockage or breaking of a blood vessel in the brain. The results may include loss of speech, paralysis, brain damage, or even death.

Tuberculosis

An infectious disease caused by a bacillus that mainly attacks the lungs. It can be acquired by drinking milk from infected cows or by breathing in the bacilli that are coughed out by other humans. These bacilli are killed by sunlight. But they can live in dust for weeks in damp and dark conditions, so bad housing encourages the spread of this disease. Poorly nourished persons are much more likely to acquire the disease than well-nourished people are. The pasteurization of milk and better sanitation are the main reasons this disease is no longer as common as it used to be.

Typhoid fever

A very infectious disease caught by eating or drinking something contaminated by the feces of someone who is infected with the typhoid fever bacillus. Humans experience a high fever, a rose-colored rash, and stomach pains. Two of Pasteur's daughters died from this disease.

Virus

A type of microorganism that can only reproduce within the body of another animal, human, or other living thing. Many types of diseases are caused by different kinds of viruses. At present there are no cures for viral diseases, so immunization remains the best means of protection. Antiviral agents, however, might someday prove effective ways of fighting viral diseases.

Yeast

A type of fungus used in the fermentation industries and in baking. Some kinds of yeasts can cause disease in humans and animals.

Chronology

1822   **December 27** — Louis Pasteur is born in Dôle, France.

1843   Louis enters the École Normale Supérieure in fourth place.

1848   **May** — Louis reads his paper on crystals to the Academy of Sciences. His mother dies at Arbois a few days later.

1849   Louis is appointed lecturer of chemistry at Strasbourg University. **May 29** — Louis marries Marie Laurent, daughter of the university rector.

1850   Their first daughter, Jeanne, is born.

1851   Their son, Jean-Baptiste, is born.

1853   Louis Pasteur is awarded the Cross of the Legion of Honor. His daughter, Cécile, is born.

1854   Louis, aged only thirty-one, is made Professor of Chemistry and Dean of the new Faculty of Sciences at Lille.

1856   Louis begins studies on fermentation.

1857   Louis becomes manager and director of scientific studies at the École Normale Supérieure in Paris.

1858   The Pasteurs' third daughter, Marie-Louise, is born.

1859   The oldest Pasteur daughter, Jeanne, dies from typhoid fever at age nine. Louis begins studies into "spontaneous generation."

1862   Louis is elected to the Academy of Sciences.

1863   The last Pasteur child, Camille, is born.

1864   **April** — Louis demonstrates the presence of germs in the air at the Sorbonne in Paris. **Summer** — Louis goes to Arbois to test wine fermentation. He discovers that heating the wine to 122-140°F (50-60°C) will prevent it from going bad; he invents pasteurization. Later he argues with other scientists about "spontaneous generation."

1865   **June** — Louis goes to Alais in southern France to investigate a disease that is killing the silkworms there. His father dies suddenly. **September** — His two-year-old daughter, Camille, dies after a long illness. **October** — A cholera epidemic breaks out; two hundred people a day are dying in Paris alone. Pasteur and his colleagues try to discover the cause, but they fail.

1866   **February** — Louis returns to Alais. Marie takes their daughters to Chambéry. **May** — Twelve-year-old Cécile dies from typhoid fever. She is buried at Arbois, as were her two sisters earlier.

1867	**July**— Louis is awarded the Grand Prix medal at the Exposition Universelle for his work on pasteurization. He is appointed professor of chemistry at the Sorbonne in Paris.
1868	**October 19** — Louis has a stroke at the age of forty-five. Though paralyzed down his left side, he refuses to stop working.
1870	The Franco-Prussian War begins. Louis publishes *Studies on the Diseases of Silkworms.*
1871	Louis starts studying beer fermentation.
1873	Louis is elected to the Academy of Medicine.
1876	Louis publishes his *Studies on Beer.*
1877	Louis begins studying anthrax after an outbreak in eastern France.
1879	During his studies on chicken cholera, Louis discovers how to immunize against disease, using weakened microbes.
1880	Louis begins his study of rabies.
1881	**June 2** — Louis' bold experiment of vaccinating sheep against anthrax is judged a complete success. He is later awarded the Grand Cordon of the Legion of Honor.
1882	Louis is elected to the Académie Française.
1885	**July 6** — Joseph Meister, bitten by a rabid dog, is brought to Louis Pasteur. Louis decides to vaccinate him, the first person ever to be vaccinated against rabies. Meister survives, and patients come from all over the world for rabies treatment.
1886	**March 1** — Louis tells the Academy of Sciences that he has treated 350 people, and only one has died of rabies. A fund is launched to build the Pasteur Institute for the treatment of rabies and the study of the transmission of disease.
1887	Louis has another stroke.
1888	**November 14** — The Pasteur Institute is officially opened.
1892	**December 27** — A great ceremony is held at the Sorbonne to recognize Louis' achievements.
1894	The Pasteur Institute succeeds in producing a vaccination for diphtheria.
1895	**September 28** — Louis dies at Villeneuve l'Etang at the age of seventy-two.

Index

air, microbes in 5-6, 10, 15, 36-38, 40-42
alcohol fermentation 25-33
anthrax 50-55
atoms 20

Balard, Antoine-Jérôme 37
beer 8, 25, 28, 33
Biot, Jean-Baptisté 20-21, 36, 37
bubonic plague 60

carbolic acid 42-44
cell division 14-15, 28, 32
Chamberland, Charles 52, 54
cholera, chicken 52-53
cholera, human 48, 51, 60
chrysalises 46
crystals 20-23, 25-27

de la Tour, Charles Cagniard 27
de Saussure, Horace Bénédict 14
diphtheria 51, 58, 60
dissymmetry 23
Duclaux, Emile 45
Dumas, Jean-Baptisté 18-20, 33, 37, 45

fermentation 25-36, 44, 50, 60
flasks, S-shaped-necked 7, 37, 40-41

germ theory 7, 10, 15, 34, 37, 41- 44, 50-52

inoculation 7, 52-58

Jenner, Edward 53
Joubert, Jules-Francois 52

Koch, Robert 50-51, 53, 60

lactic acid 29, 31-32
Leeuwenhoek, Anton van 10-12, 28
Lister, Joseph 42- 44, 59

Metchnikov, Elie 58
microscope, invention of 10-11

Pasteur Institute 58, 60
Pasteur, Louis
    Academy of Medicine, elected to 52

Barbet boarding school 18
Besançon, college in 18
birth and childhood 17
children
    birth of 24
    death of 40, 48
death 58-60
École Normale Supérieure, Administrator
    and Director of Scientific Studies 33
father of 17
Lille Faculty of Sciences, dean and
    professor of chemistry 24
Lycée St. Louis 18
marries Marie Laurent 23-24
mother of 17
school in Paris 18-23
sisters 17
Sorbonne, the 18-19, 40
Strasbourg, University of, lecturer in
    chemistry 23
strokes 48, 58
pasteurization 8, 33, 42
pébrine 45- 46

rabies 55-58
Redi, Francesco 14
rods, microscopic 14, 28-32, 51
Roux, Emile 24, 52, 54, 58, 60

silkworms 8, 45-50
smallpox 53, 60
Spallanzani, Lazzaro 13-14, 28, 33, 36
spontaneous generation 13-15, 33-40, 50
stereochemistry 22

Thuillier, Louis 54
typhoid fever 40, 48, 54, 60

vaccination 52-58
vaccines 52-58, 60
vinegar 24, 33
viruses 55, 60

wine 8 -10, 21, 25, 33, 42

yeast 27-33, 50
Yersin, Alexandre 58, 60